SPOUSE CARING FOR EACH OTHER

TIPS TO BE YOUR SPOUSE'S BEST FRIEND AND STRENGTHEN YOUR MARRIAGE

By

Abraham Shrub

TABLE OF CONTENTS

CHAPTER 1

DEALING WITH EACH OTHER IN MARRIAGE-MIND, BODY, AND SPIRIT

Dealing with one another as it connects with the body basically implies you are empowering each other to be dynamic, eat soundly, get appropriate rest, and look for clinical consideration when essential. Actual contact in marriage is significant .Making sure that your life partner isn't yearning for actual contact is one more method for dealing with them genuinely.

Marriage can turn out to be progressively troublesome as life becomes standard for couples. Many couples disregard themselves and each other as they make work, bringing up youngsters, church, and different commitments beyond their marriage a need.

We disregard ourselves and each other for some reasons, yet the most widely recognized and most clear reasons are we end our own lives and mortality for conceded, and expect we and our companions will constantly be near.

The fact of the matter is our own well-being and Sprosperity ought not be required to be postponed while we deal with all the other things and every other person, nor should our relationships.

Married people also tend to neglect the care of themselves or each other as a result of an ongoing conflict.

CHAPTER 2

UNSETTLED CLASHES LEAD TO EVASION IN MARRIAGE

At the point when there is continuous and unsettled struggle in a marriage evasion normally occurs.

Most people try not to converse with their companion because of the trepidation that discussing it or bringing it up will worthy motivation another contention. With evasion comes a distance, and with distance comes to absence of understanding and information.

For instance, assuming that you are staying away from your companion since you dread another conflict is unavoidable while your life partner is managing disease, stress at work or injury, or any sort of physical or profound side effects, you might wind up in obscurity about your mate's condition.

At the point when your mate feels associated with you they are bound to share their everyday feelings, difficulties, triumphs, and encounters with you.

At the point when one accomplice has been depressed long haul because of continuous struggle or different reasons, it powers their life partner to smother sentiments, side effects, contemplation, and encounters.

On occasion one could feel their main choice is to impart them to another person who may be genuinely accessible and keen on catching wind of how they are doing consistently. At last, they could start to feel more associated with this external individual (typically a colleague, companion, neighbor, or somebody they met on the web).

This opens the entryway for one or the two players to turn out to be genuinely appended to somebody other than their mate.

Dealing with one another is perhaps of the main obligation in a marriage, and on the off chance that you are continuously battling, or separated, repressed it is difficult to satisfactorily fulfill this obligation.

Time after time an issue, a clinical emergency, or a crisis interferes with this constant pattern of contention, evasion, and inability to remain sincerely accessible.

Sadly, many couples don't recognize the degree to which they have underestimated each other until such an occasion has happened.

CHAPTER 3

COMPREHEND TIME IS VALUABLE

Reconnecting and understanding that time is significant preceding any clinical emergency or hazardous conditions are the most ideal decision.

This is probably going to forestall such emergencies or crises, as being in line with one another everyday will improve the probability that one will see changes in their companions' state of mind, conduct, or prosperity and urge them to look for essential treatment or administrations.

Moreover, when there is no distinction among a couple, the probability of being powerless against unfaithfulness is diminished.

An individual is more averse to deal with oneself in the event that they don't have friends and family who care and are focusing near, particularly men.

It's undeniably true that -

Hitched men live longer than men who aren't hitched.

This implies that when you're not dealing with one another, you are more averse to deal with yourselves as people. This could bring about decay in generally speaking mental and actual wellbeing.

Dealing with one another as it connects with the body essentially implies you are empowering each other to be dynamic, eat steadily, get appropriate rest, and look for clinical consideration when vital.

CHAPTER 4

IMPORTANT PYSICAL CONTACT IN MARRIAGE

Ensuring that your companion isn't yearning for actual contact is one more method for dealing with them truly.

As people, we as a whole lengthy for actual contact and the chance to practice and use our feeling of touch. It is silly for any wedded person to get themselves yearning for this or to feel like this isn't a possibility for them.

Nobody gets hitched guessing that they will be denied and kept from human touch or potentially actual contact.

Sadly, frequently this happens frequently in marriage. Every individual ought to feel they can uninhibitedly utilize each of the five of your faculties in their union with feel, give, and get love.

Actual contact isn't restricted to however incorporates sex.

Alternate ways one can ensure their mate doesn't wind up starving for human contact is by clasping hands, kissing, sitting on one another lap, snuggling, shoulder rubs, taps on the posterior, embraces, and delicate kisses on the neck or different pieces of the body.

Delicately scouring your mate's leg, head, arm, or back is additionally successful.

All things considered, who could do without to lay on their mates' chest and experience the glow of their hand tenderly rub their head, back, or arm?

This is very soothing to most yet can turn into an unfamiliar type of fondness in relationships in the event that it won't ever happen.

When it becomes unfamiliar or new, it very well may be awkward for you or your companion for the initial not many times. The objective ought to be to make this a normal, recognizable, and agreeable piece of love in your marriage.

CHAPTER 5

SHARED ASSUMPTIONS CAN LESSEN ISSUES IN MARRIAGE

Sex is a significant piece of closeness in marriage, more so for some than others.

One misstep individuals make in relationships is neglecting to look at whether as an actual touch is as vital to their mate for what it's worth for them.

On the off chance that one party sees different types of closeness more significant and their accomplice sees the genuine actual demonstration of sex as most significant, this can become dangerous in the event that they can't have a solid exchange about it and plan as needs be.

Examine this and sort out how you can oblige each other's actual necessities and wants with the goal that neither one of the feels denied of what they consider significant.

Dealing with yourself and your life partner as it connects with mind and additionally feelings can be complicated since our distinction in needs is perplexing.

Hitched couples should offer profound help for one another, and should see each other's close to home contrasts and needs first.

CHAPTER 6

COMMUNICATION IN MARRIAGE CREATES A HEALTHY BONDING

CORRESPONDENCE SHOULD BE SOLID.

For instance, understanding that ladies and men impart diversely is a vital piece of ensuring correspondence and move were made in this space are solid and sufficient.

There are consistently special cases for the standard yet by and large, ladies need to convey all the more habitually and to a greater extent. What's more, men need to have a solid sense of security enough with their life partner to be defenseless by conveying their sentiments.

They need to realize that what they share will not be in some way utilized against them in a future conflict or conversation.

One more method for guaranteeing you are taking care of one another feelings by guaranteeing correspondence is solid in a marriage is by ensuring you are imparting all the more much of the time as well as ensuring the substance of the conversation is significant, deliberate, and gainful.

Discussing the weather conditions will not do. Inquire as to whether they accept they are not being dealt with in any space and how they accept you might address this shortfall.

Examine ways that you accept you and your life partner could add to making your marriage better, more tomfoolery, and really satisfying. As I expressed before, ensure struggle doesn't go unsettled as this is harmful to the marriage and obstructs correspondence.

You will find it very challenging to have significant and incessant correspondence or actual contact assuming that you have weeks, months, or long periods of unsettled struggle.

CHAPTER 7

THE FEELING OF PERSONALITY AND DISTINCTION FORESTALLS UNDESIRABLE SORROWS AND NERVES

The most ideal option for our companions in a genuine way isn't anticipating that they should be our God.

For instance, we as a whole have profound requirements that another human can't fulfill, for example, the requirement for reason and character.

Anticipating that your life partner should be your motivation or the main explanation you get up toward the beginning of the day is risky in light of multiple factors.

One explanation is this just isn't their obligation as your mate. Another profound need your companion couldn't really satisfy is the requirement for a feeling of character.

At the point when we permit our union with be our personality and we have no clue about who we are beyond the marriage we put ourselves positioned for profound sadness, absence of satisfaction, nervousness, a poisonous marriage, and that's only the tip of the iceberg.

Your marriage ought to be a piece of what your identity is, not exclusively what your identity is.

In the event that you end up being compelled to live without your companion sometime in the future, and you end up with no personality and no feeling of direction, you could battle to track down motivations to live, become seriously discouraged, or more regrettable.

These profound necessities must be satisfied by you and your higher power.

On the off chance that you don't put stock in God or you don't have a more powerful you should burrow down profound and fulfill these necessities or track down solid ways of satisfying them.

Assuming you have a disengaged or disappointed outlook on the condition of your marriage yet need to stay away from partition or potentially separate, the marriage.com course implied for wedded couples is a magnificent asset to assist you with defeating the most difficult parts of being hitched.

CHAPTER 8

WHAT KIND OF SUPPORT DO SPOUSES NEED FROM EACH OTHER?

After two individuals wed, they are probably going to look for a kind of help from one another that they didn't try similarly prior to wedding.

From research wedded couples put a high top notch on their accomplices' help of anything they decide to be important commitments. Hitched individuals need their mate's help for satisfying their obligations and meeting their responsibilities.

Before individuals wed, they will generally zero in substantially more on supporting each other in objectives that are future-situated than on objectives connected with the security and upkeep of their coexistence. Drawn in couples may not think how emphatically they will require each other's help after they wed for arriving at objectives, yet for keeping up with the security of their coexistence.

"Individuals intending to get hitched ought to ponder not just the way that their accomplices support what they desire to accomplish yet in addition about how their accomplices support what they feel committed to achieve. We could wind up with both more joyful relationships and more fulfilled individuals overall.

Preceding wedding, individuals go to one another for help in the profound promising and less promising times of life and during seasons of pressure. They likewise need each other's help for arriving at long haul objectives and accomplishing their fantasies. Hitched individuals actually look for that sort of help from one another yet that their prosperity requests one more sort of help also.

couples wanting to marry would do well to examine the need they will have as a wedded couple for this kind of help, maybe in a marriage-planning program.

Many couples "don't unexpectedly ponder whether their accomplice upholds their satisfaction of obligations and commitments while choosing to wed. So I truly do feel that something maybe ought to be to a greater degree a concentration in early directing.

For instance assuming two individuals were asked exclusively "to portray what they felt their essential obligations were both inside and beyond the relationship and afterward whether they feel their accomplice upholds them in achieving those obligations, this would give a thought of whether that kind of help is there. Assuming it were deficient with regards to, couples could be urged to ponder how their accomplice might further develop support around here."

Prior to wedding, "couples could be urged to ponder whether their accomplice is somebody who won't just be ready for the drawn out expectations and yearnings they have set for themselves, yet who will likewise appreciate and aid the more quick obligations they accept they should oversee from one day to another".

CHAPTER 9

11 EASY WAYS TO SHOW YOUR SPOUSE THAT YOU CARE

In the midst of the bustling surge of our regular day to day existences, it's not difficult to get overpowered by every one of our errands for every day, and it turns out to be not entirely obvious the necessities of each of the others in our family. At the point when we are continually pondering our long plan for the day for the following day, days, weeks, and months can go by without recognizing our accomplices other than a short discussion over supper and just before sleep time.

know in our home, the children hit the sack soon after my better half returns home from work. So we have supper and quickly begin into the children's sleep time schedule, while never having any time together. The main time we truly get to try and converse with one another without interference is if we both incidentally turn out to be alert in the late hours of the night after the children have headed to sleep, and we have both completed the process of chipping away at our singular organizations. We need to put forth a deliberate attempt consistently and consistently to ensure we are showing the other individual we give it a second thought and recognizing their requirements, regardless of whether that implies chatting on the telephone over my better half's noon and after my most youthful child's naptime.

In this day in age, where more hours are expected working to bring in a similar measure of cash, getting your bills paid consistently as a rule takes two salaries, and your time is brilliant, it's a higher priority than at any other time to exceed everyone's expectations to show your life partner that you care to keep a solid marriage/relationship. Furthermore, when you have kids, this is much more significant as they are realizing being a man or a lady, and being seeing someone, their folks. Assuming they see their folks as two individuals that are exceptionally tender and love each other definitely, regardless of whether the two of them need to make a solid effort to keep the family running, they are bound to find a sound relationship that models yours themselves when they are more established.

Be that as it may, how might you show your companion you care without investing a lot of energy and cash, the two of which are rare nowadays? Incredible inquiry! We should take a gander at a simple methods for showing your life partner that you give it a second thought.

CHAPTER 10

LET THEM KNOW HOW MUCH YOU LOVE THEM

TELL HIM OR HER FREQUENTLY

Literally nothing shows that you care about somebody more than truly saying the words "I love you." Now I don't mean aimlessly rehashing it to the next individual's calling of affection, or expressing it with an eye roll or a moan. For it to truly have power, ensure that you are looking at the other individual in the eye, holding their hands on the off chance that conceivable, grinning, and saying it.

And afterward, much more critically, follow your calling of adoration up with activity. Have you heard the colloquialism "Talk is cheap"? It's valid! On the off chance that you say it however at that point don't show them that you mean it with cherishing activities, it loses its significance. Fortunately, I have recorded 10 additional magnificent things you can DO to show your life partner, with activity, that you genuinely would not joke about this.

I'm not saying you will not have occupied days, or awful days, where you won't feel so cherishing, and that is totally fine. However, endeavor to show your adoration genuinely a greater number of days than not. They'll receive the message. A relationship is around two individuals cooperating to help the other. However long you are regularly conveying your adoration, particularly when it is required the most, and afterward finishing your activities, you are looking great so far.

SPEAK POSITIVELY ABOUT THE OTHER IN FRONT OF YOUR KIDS

The manner in which you talk about your mate before your children has a lot greater effect than you would accept. Talking adversely about the other parent to your children can really impact not just the manner in which they ponder the other parent however the manner in which they treat them also. Fortunately, talking emphatically can also. Let your children know what a brilliant mother they have, how hard she attempts to keep the family running, and that they ought to give their very best for help her around the house, and she'll see it and feel it in the manner they treat her.

Converse with your children about how hard daddy attempts to accommodate the family, the amount he adores you and his children, and urge them to be cherishing and steady when he returns home from work, and he will observer your affection through your children. By treating your mate with affection and regard around your children, they will get that equivalent experience, as well as feeling a conviction that all is good at home and with their folks.

The manner in which you train them to see their mother and father can likewise shape the manner in which they view the other gender in ongoing connections, and how they go about as a mother or father from here on out.

Assuming they accept all men are lethargic and pointless, for example, or all ladies are annoys, how does that help their view representing things to come in connections? Train them to see the best in one another and approach others with deference and love and you're giving them the establishment for their own connections while building your own

CHAPTER 11

ACCOMPLISH SOMETHING SPECIAL JUST BECAUSE

Love is really focusing on someone else and their bliss over your own. What's more, this is one approach to show that to someone else genuinely. Anyway this expects you to step beyond your own contemplations once in a while to see what might truly be useful or show the other individual you give it a second thought. On the off chance that you see that he is attempting to get a decent lunch made for work consistently, or goes out without a good breakfast every morning, perhaps you could save something for him the prior night when you consider it, that would make his morning simpler

CHAPTER 12

TIPS TO BE YOUR SPOUSE'S BEST FRIEND AND STRENGTHEN YOUR MARRIAGE

In the event that you see the dishes or clothing piling up each day, and she's looking truly worn out, think about placing in a heap for her without saying anything. I guarantee nothing says love like a vacant sink, or an unfilled clothing bushel. Perhaps these ideas are a lot for the time being you have. That doesn't imply that you were unable to draw a directive for them on the washroom reflect for them to figure out the following opportunity they scrub down, or pass on them a treat on the counter to find when they get out.

Fixing something they've been battling with, or cleaning something that is a big deal to them, similar to the vehicle or the room would likewise have a major effect. It doesn't need to be large to show you give it a second thought, it simply must be unique, and don't let them know you made it happen. That works everything out such that exceptional.

LEAVE A SPECIAL NOTE

By leaving a note, I didn't mean it must be a gigantic showcase, yet the way that great would you feel to get back home to this on the entryway, it positively would make you can't help thinking about the thing was sitting tight for you inside. I consider one the things I love the most about my better half is the little notes he passes on me to find in the first part of the day when I get up with the children. Whether it's a composed note of conciliatory sentiment, a portrayal of his appreciation for me, or even an entertaining little I love you some place in the house, they are totally valued.

Recently my husband left me a drawing of an eye, a heart, and a sheep to say he cherished me. It was magnificent. What might work for your companion, a note in his lunch or folder case, a major cut-out heart in the cooler for her to find, Maybe a heart drawn on the restroom reflect for the other to find, One evening I came higher up to give the child a rest and work on my blog, and my better half had stapled a wonderful, empowering statement over my PC for me to find.

Around here, a small amount makes a huge difference to communicating your sentiments. What might be significant to your companion?

SAY THANK YOU

How frequently do we endeavor to show somebody we give it a second thought and nothing is by all accounts fulfilling them? When did you last say much obliged? I incidentally turn out to be a homemaker, and I realize that in the wake of really buckling down attempting to fight the children, work on self-teaching, keeping the house perfect, the dishes and clothing done, work on my business and keep everybody took care of the entire day, including a scrumptious supper, I'm cleaned.

On the off chance that my better half returns home from work and doesn't see any of the endeavors I put into holding the house back from torching consistently, a large number of days, I get somewhat angry. I do whatever it takes not to, yet once in a while it seems like I'm in isolation in my endeavors to deal with my family and keep everybody blissful. Furthermore, guess what? My better half feels the same way. He starts off ahead of schedule and gets back home late; he buckles down the entire day to cover our bills and put food on the table, meanwhile passing up investing energy with his loved ones. On the off chance that I never consider this, and say nothing, he begins to feel angry.

In some cases, some straightforward appreciation and affirmation of the work with respect to your life partner can improve things greatly. Particularly assuming it seems like nothing else is working, attempt "thank you for all that you do to deal with us".

TRY TO BE POSITIVE

Inspiration is infectious, as is pessimism. Welcome your mate by the day's end happily, discuss all that you must be appreciative for, be empowering and elevating, see what is happening, and you'll begin seeing a similar in the person in question. It's discouraging to be pessimistic, and it's depleting for the other individual. Nobody needs to must be the one continuously pulling the other back from the edge, persuading them regarding life's worth, and making the best of each and every circumstance without anyone else.

So ensure that you are adding to looking forward with trust, appreciating the present, and laying out objectives for what's in store. It truly doesn't make any difference which side you ordinarily fall on, in light of the fact that energy will in general spread significantly further. You will have awful days, and that is the point at which the other individual ought to move forward to make up for the shortcoming and be empowering and strong, yet somebody needs to kick it off.

Lift up your relationship, make the other individual great when you're near, and be a signal in obscurity, and when you want it, you'll get that equivalent cherishing support.

SEND A TEXT AROUND MID-AFTERNOON

You probably realize how occupied you get during the day, paying little heed to what calling you're in. Perhaps you likewise get overpowered, baffled, drained, deterred, or furious. How much would it mean in the event that somebody you cherished sent you a decent message about how great you were, Or the amount you were adored, What in the event that you received a message in your most disappointing day saying your #1 dinner would be sitting tight for you at home.

Everybody likes to realize they are important to another person. I think it carries a grin to basically everybody's face to realize that somebody is contemplating them and cares. Far superior, the perfect message could in fact separate a distressing day and turn it around to improve things. I know how I feel when the right message comes from my better half in the center of a hard and fast implosion. Yet, it's similarly as magnificent to realize I'm cherished during the tranquil snapshots of my day.

Be the one that carries a grin to your mate's face around mid-afternoon. Cause that person to feel cherished, appreciated, and important, and you'll be the one they go to for security and trust from now on. Marriage is intended to be where you can track down solace and backing. You are wedding your sidekick, the individual who can make you grin, and your associate, right, treat them that way and you'll fortify your relationship with each word you type or each image you send.

CHAPTER 13

WELCOME HIM OR HER WITH ENTHUSIASM

Something I've seen when I make an appearance to get my most seasoned youngster from Sunday school, is that his face illuminates, he gets a tremendous grin, and he comes running for me. I love it, and I really won't let any other person go get him due to how great it feels to be welcomed that way. At the point when my better half returns home from work, he gets that equivalent reaction from our two children shouting "Daddy's home!"

On the off chance that you realize that somebody was hanging tight for you at home with a tremendous grin and an embrace, couldn't you additionally anticipate that feeling consistently as I do getting my child from Sunday school? Obviously you would! Everybody needs to realize they are adored and esteemed some place. I additionally love when my significant other strolls in the entryway. As a matter of fact I could most likely leave it at that yet when he has a grin all over and says he's been anticipating seeing me the entire day, it truly doesn't make any difference how the day went. My entire night has been made.

Give your mate that gift as frequently as you can and you may very well see him returning home a piece early consistently or have something exceptional sitting tight for you when you return home. Welcome your band together with energy toward the finish of each and every day and you'll see a lot more joyful life partner.

CHAPTER 14

ENDEAVOR TO ACCOMPLISH MORE THAN YOUR HALF

Such countless individuals say that connections are around 50/50. Every individual gives half and the relationship works. Truly, so what happens when I'm just inclination 20% today or he can give 10%? Who compensates for any shortfall?

I accept that solid connections are 100/100. Everybody does everything they possibly can for deal with the other individual. There will be days when I can't give 100 percent and that is OK, since I have somebody in my life that can fill in the hole for me, as well as the other way around. There are numerous days when every one of us is putting forth a valiant effort it actually isn't sufficient. There's something else to do, more bills to pay, more consideration that our children need, and not anywhere close to sufficient rest, and on those days, we convey one another.

That makes me consider the stage in our lives when my firstborn was pristine. He would not rest by any means, ever and would keep us conscious the entire evening causing a scene. Every one of us would alternate strolling him, attempting to sort out some way to inspire him to rest, while scarcely having the option to walk ourselves. He would walk him around until he was running into walls from weariness, and afterward it was my chance to do likewise. I didn't figure both of us would make due, yet here we are 4 years after the fact with another little one (that loves to rest, thank heavens.

We made it, and we've endured all that life has thrown our direction, since even in our most vulnerable times, we both upheld one another. Occasionally will require a greater amount of you while you support your life partner, however realize that it works the two different ways and you'll require your mate to pull all the weight one day as well. Endeavor to allow 100 percent consistently. It will pay off.

BE EMPOWERING

You and your mate are two totally various individuals that have come from totally various foundations. At the point when you came into the relationship, you each had your own fantasies and wants. My fantasy had forever been to be a distributed creator and a housewife.

CHAPTER 15

MAKE OBJECTIVES FOR YOUR FUTURE TOGETHER

At the point when you love somebody, you envision coexistence with them later on. What sort of dreams do you both have together, Do you both need to venture to the far corners of the planet, begin a ranch, or become guardians. What sort of future objectives could you at any point set that could permit you to cooperate towards a typical objective

My significant other and I have both needed to live on some land and raise harvests and creatures. We discussed this on our most memorable date. Consistently we've been together we've examined how we were pursuing that objective and what our timetable for that was. It has been the subject of our entire relationship and, surprisingly, the light toward the finish of numerous dim passages. This year, this month, could at long last be our chance to see that work out following 10 years together.

What is driving you? What holds you together and keeps you both propelled in difficult stretches in your lives. By making objectives together for the future, you are let your companion know that you need the person in question in your life for the long stretch. Having a joint dream assists the two individuals in the relationship with feeling like they aren't in this enormous insane world together, yet rather have an accomplice. According to it, "I love you and believe that should do this large thing called existence with you until the end of time. I have a fantasy and I maintain that should do it with you."

MAKE OBJECTIVES TOGETHER

This is the individual that you decided to focus on until the end of your life for more extravagant or less fortunate, in ailment and in wellbeing. Such countless couples are getting separated of late on the grounds that they are letting their everyday timetables, and their craving to satisfy their own requirements, without respect for the other individual, impede their obligation and obligation to their life partner. It tends to be very satisfying to cherish someone else and be adored in kind.

However, you need to really try, as it's not about to happen completely all alone.

Regardless of whether you took only a couple of recommendations from this article, you'd do far more than many individuals do in their connections today. Similarly as you appreciate (and daresay need to) feeling adored, acknowledged, and esteemed, so does your life partner. I think the best thing I have at any point perused concerning working on your relationship with a friend or family member, is to treat them with the adoration and regard you want. The most you feel like something is off-base, and you don't feel adored, that is the ideal second to be living and show your adoration to the next individual. Almost certainly, they are in a comparable situation.

Where a great many people would pull away and attempt to cause the other individual to feel something very similar, making a tremendous break in your relationship, you can be unique. Be thoughtful, be adoring, and attempt to comprehend. Would could it be that you could like most while feeling disliked and overlooked? That is how you ought to do the other individual. Furthermore, I bet you get the gigantic reward of returning that equivalent love and grasping back to you. Individuals that vibe cherished need to be adored back. Decide to show your companion the amount you care by picking one of these extraordinary simple ways. You'll be appreciative you did!

I had the open door right off the bat in our relationship to step back and begin composing and my better half upheld me 100 percent. However at that point came his time. He needed to move to one more state to seek after his helicopter flying permit, and think about what... we went. I'm not saying that you need to do whatever emotional to strong and empower. Be that as it may, you ought to maintain that your companion should be the best individual they can be.

If they have any desire to eat better, attempt to be empowering and oblige it. If they have any desire to begin practicing more, why not go do it with them? You might uphold their fantasies and wants by praising them on their aspiration, giving them an opportunity to seek after their longings, and keep awake to date on any headway they make. Be a venturing stone and not a hindrance.

CHAPTER 16

THE MOST EFFECTIVE METHOD TO REALLY CHERISH YOUR COMPANION

Genuine romance, the sort of affection that holds a couple together for a lifetime, isn't an inclination yet a demeanor. According to it, "With the assistance of God, I will give my very best for upgrade the existence of my companion."

He sat in my office and said, "I simply don't cherish my better half any longer. I wish I did, yet I don't. I've even requested that God give me love for her. Be that as it may, I simply have no affections for her any longer."

This spouse was totally true, however he was off track in how he might interpret love. He envisioned love as warm, profound, heartfelt affections for his significant other.

Since these didn't exist, he was unable to make them and even God was not giving them, he inferred that his marriage was finished. Large number of people in our general public have arrived at a similar resolution.

Genuine romance, the sort of adoration that holds a couple together for a lifetime, isn't an inclination however a disposition. According to it, With the assistance of God, I will give my very best for upgrade the existence of my mate.

This disposition prompts words and activities that are useful to your life partner and frequently animate warm feelings inside the mate's heart. Assuming this individual responds with words and conduct that express their affection for you, warm feelings may likewise get back to you.

One of the extraordinary misfortunes of Western culture is that we have likened love with warm close to home sentiments. Truth be told, these warm heartfelt sentiments are the consequence of adoration, not the substance of affection. For this reason love can be instructed. Fortunately anything that God orders, He empowers us to do.

LOVE AS A LIFESTYLE

Some say love is a demonstration of kindness. That isn't absolutely obvious. Individuals can do a valuable activity with a heartless mentality.

The spouse who says with a cruel voice, "Alright, I'll take the trash out in the event that you will ease up" has not played out a demonstration of affection.

The spouse who takes care of the lawn basically in light of the fact that his significant other has been pestering him for a really long time is doing a thoughtful demonstration, yet quieting her basic words might be finished.

The spouse who consents to be physically personal with her significant other just out of obligation or culpability isn't playing out a demonstration of affection, all things considered.

Love is the decision to help out God in serving your mate. The people who really love consider themselves to be God's representatives for enhancing the existences of their marriage accomplice. For their purposes, love is a lifestyle. They are continually searching for ways of empowering, and support the accomplice.

Such love frequently animates warm, heartfelt sentiments in the core of the companion. Feelings are the good to beat all. Be that as it may, without a caring demeanor and suitable way of behaving, the icing will soften.

God needs to involve you in your marriage. Request that he give you a caring disposition toward your companion and to spill out His adoration through you. It is a request God will reply.

CHAPTER 17

WHEN CARING FOR A SICK SPOUSE SHAKES A MARRIAGE TO THE CORE

RESET ASSUMPTIONS.

Couples need to confront what is being lost because of sickness and, simultaneously, center around what stays in one piece.

EVENLY DIVIDE LIABILITIES:

Couples need to hold a feeling of equilibrium in their connections, to the degree conceivable. Frequently this is undermined as one companion turns out to be less ready to work and different takes on additional obligations.

INCLUDE THE ILL SPOUSE

Avoid assigning the ill spouse to a passive role of being "cared for." To the extent possible, set boundaries around caregiving and maintain reciprocity in the relationship.

EXTEND YOUR ORGANIZATION:

In the event that loved ones don't appear to comprehend what you're going through, find individuals who do. Well and sick life partners might have to track down help in better places.

Make significance: sooner or later, you must have the option to make importance of what you're going through as a guardian and integrate this into another feeling of character.

For some individuals, significance rotates around the thought of "devotion" - obligation to their mate, their commitments and the "we" of their relationship, he said.

CHAPTER 18

THE MOST EFFECTIVE METHOD TO SAFEGUARD THE MARRIAGE BOND WHILE CARING FOR THE SPOUSE

MOVE AWAY FROM THE FIGHT

With any conjugal conflict, in the event that each accomplice is completely persuaded of the rightness of their perspective and keen on demonstrating the misleading quality of the other's, little correspondence or

COMPROMISE IS CONCEIVABLE:

As their fight seethes, they harm the groundwork of trust whereupon all enduring connections should be based. Couples need to withdraw from the battle to the point of thinking about why it is happening. Once in a while this requires an outsider, like a guide or specialist or pastor /imam, to quiet matters and proposition bits of knowledge.

RETHINK DIVISION OF WORK

When sickness strikes, the relationship is quite often on a very basic level changed. Be that as it may, companions can limit those changes on the off chance that they find manners by which the two accomplices can contribute.

Be careful: That is the case regardless of whether the well life partner thinks (legitimately or not) that it would be simpler and quicker to do everything himself.

REESTABLISH THE DELIGHT

What unites two individuals to turn into a couple isn't by and large misfortune or drudgery however having a good time. For accomplices adapting to disease, that actually should be a significant focal point of their cooperations. Sorting out what they can partake in together, notwithstanding, may require a little preparation.

CHAPTER 19

BOUNDARIES

At the point when you wed somebody, you assume the weight of cherishing your mate profoundly and really focusing on that person concerning no other. You care about what you mean for your life partner; you care about your mate's government assistance and sentiments. On the off chance that one mate feels no awareness of others' expectations to the next, this companion is, as a result, attempting to carry on with wedded life as a solitary individual. Then again, you can't go too far of obligation. You want to try not to take possession for your mate's life.

CHAPTER 20

THE LAW OF OBLIGATION IN MARRIAGE

We are mindful to one another, however not for one another. The word trouble shows a backbreaking stone, for example, a monetary, well-being, or profound emergency.

Companions effectively support each other when one is worrying about a staggering concern. The term load, nonetheless, demonstrates one's everyday obligations of life. This incorporates one's sentiments, perspectives, values, and treatment of life's ordinary hardships. Companions might help each other out with loads, at the end of the day, every individual should deal with his own day to day liabilities.

Two limits happen in marriage when the law of obligation isn't complied. From one perspective, a spouse will disregard his obligation to cherish his significant other. He might become self centered, impolite, or terrible. He won't consider how his activities influence and impact his mate. This is being flighty to a life partner.

Then again, a spouse might assume on liability his significant other ought to bear. For instance, his significant other might be troubled, and he might feel liable for her joy. Maybe he feels that he isn't bringing in sufficient cash, showing sufficient premium in her exercises, or aiding sufficient around the house. So he endlessly attempts to fulfill a miserable individual. This is an unthinkable undertaking. While a spouse ought to be thoughtful toward his miserable wife and assume a sense of ownership with his own pernicious way of behaving, he shouldn't get a sense of ownership with her sentiments. They are hers, and she should deal with them herself.

Couples have an obligation to draw certain lines on every mate's horrendous demonstrations or mentalities. For instance, assuming a spouse has a betting issue, his better half necessities to draw proper lines, for example, dropping his Visas, isolating their shared services, or demanding that he get proficient assistance, to drive him to get a sense of ownership with his concern. The law of obligation in marriage implies that companions won't save or empower the wicked or youthful way of behaving of their accomplices.

Whether you're a love bird or hitched for a long time, figure out how Limits in Marriage will assist you with building an establishment for your relationship to prosper

CHAPTER 21
DUTY OF A WIFE

Marriage changes the existence of a lady; from a spoiled lighthearted young lady, she develops into a capable spouse prepared to assume the obligations of a wife. We should find out what those obligations are:

LOVE HIM GENUINELY

In a marriage, a man needs to be enjoyed, cherished, and valued very much like a lady does. As a spouse, give unqualified love to your significant other truly and inwardly. Value him liberally and support him as your kid. Furthermore, what do you receive consequently, His genuine love, obviously.

HELP HIM

Who said men don't require help, we all need assistance and backing. Turn into your better half's assistance during difficult stretches. Whenever he looks for your assistance, be proactive in supporting him. He will do the equivalent when you need his support.

Keep his honor/poise: Don't talk negative about your significant other to your family, companions, or family members. Try not to battle with him or reprimand him before others. Try not to enjoy blabbering about your better half. Assuming that you have any issues, figure it out among you.

Support him: A spouse ought to remain by her better half and work all together. Whether it is everyday schedules or accomplishing long haul objectives, you really want to help your significant other in the entirety of his endeavors and attempts. He will love to have you next to him in each step he takes.

BE ACCESSIBLE

A spouse needs her significant other's organization, and a husband needs his better half's. Show up for him when he needs to converse with you. Pay attention to him and prompt him whenever required, and deal with his necessities. It shows that you love and care for him.

REGARD HIM

Regard is common. Esteem his perspectives and regard him for what he is. On the off chance that you can't help contradicting him, don't affront him however put across your point delicately. At the point when you give regard, you gain appreciation.

SATISFY HIS REQUIREMENTS

Cook for him, deal with him when he is unwell or inspire his mind-set when he is worried, very much like he satisfies your necessities.

Be devoted to your significant other: When hitched, you need to stay steadfast and focused on your significant other, regardless. Try not to give him degree to scrutinize your dedication. Also, anticipate something very similar from him.

Look for his perspective: When you look for your better half's viewpoint, it doesn't make you any lesser. It shows you esteem his perspective and regard him, truth be told.

Cook for him: Dish out good dinners for your better half as well as you. Keep away from the allurement of getting a good unhealthy food en route to work. You might request that your significant other assistance you in the kitchen, and that could be an effective method for investing more energy with one another.

Regard your parents in law: Independent of the distinctions in culture or way of life, regard them as they are your in-laws; you could maintain that your better half should regard your folks, couldn't you?

DEAL WITH FAMILY OBLIGATIONS:

Keep the house all together, clean and clean. Look for help from your better half and youngsters. Apportion them a few obligations to do consistently. Along these lines, every individual feels dependable towards their part in the family.

BE MINDFUL

Being a capable spouse is a gift to the family since she understands what to do and how to do. Be capable in running the family, dealing with your funds, and dealing with your youngsters.

Show restraint: Persistence doesn't come without any problem. At the point when you are performing multiple tasks consistently with your obligations at home, and things don't go as you plan, the last thing you ponder is tolerance. In any case, take a stab at having it and you won't think twice about it. Envision, you are in a rush to race to work, your better half asks you something senseless and you impact him. In any case, later in the day, you understand that he was simply attempting to be perky with you. Had you been more persistent in the first part of the day, the day would have been exceptional both for yourself as well as your better half.

Teach your youngsters: Nurturing is an obligation of both the mother and father. Yet, a mother assumes a huge part in teaching her kids, as she comprehends them back to front, and has the persistence and time to sit with them.

DEFEND YOUR HOME

You should shield your home from outsiders and individuals who attempt to infuse venomous contemplation in your relatives. You ought to likewise ward off yourself from people who have a great deal of cynicism in them.

DEAL WITH YOURSELF

No, this isn't the last thing to do. Truth be told, you ought to zero in on yourself before you deal with others in light of the fact that your family can be cheerful and sound provided that you are blissful and solid. Try not to trouble yourself with obligations. Look for help from the others in the family, enjoy some time off and unwind. This will keep you grinning and a grinning spouse will be the most satisfying thing to see for a husband.

CHAPTER 22

REGULARLY SOUGHT CLARIFICATION ON SOME PRESSING ISSUES

A spouse ought to treat her significant other with affection and regard. A decent spouse is her significant other's closest companion, guide, pundit, and team promoter. Along these lines, repeat your affection and show you care for him through your activities.

Loan him a listening ear when he needs to talk and encourage him when he feels down. Be sincerely accessible, urge him to seek after his fantasies and ensure you generally have him covered.

HOW TO BE A CAPABLE SPOUSE

Attempt to grasp your better half and acknowledge him how he is. Find opportunity to instantly convey your considerations and sentiments and iron out contrasts. Disregard unreasonable assumptions and keep things light.

CHAPTER 23

TOP 10 CHARACTERISTICS OF A GOOD HUSBAND

The following are a portion of the top characteristics that a spouse ought to have -

•HE OUGHT TO BE RELIABLE

The spouse should have the option to trust in him and furthermore realize that he adores her just and not another person. Men are truly adept at dating, however with regards to being a decent spouse, they more than frequently come up short. Men who have a sexual involvement in numerous ladies in the past are less inclined to be dedicated to their spouses. It is like individuals leaving liquor, where a high level of individuals fall flat. The sentiment present while dating gradually blurs and it is restricted to pretty much just while fornication.

•FAITHFULNESS IS EXCEPTIONALLY FUNDAMENTAL

A spouse can never impart her man to another lady and anticipates that her significant other should be faithful to her. Frequently, the spouse strays, and this causes a lot of strain and grinding in the family. A spouse might decide to excuse, and on the off chance that the undertaking with the other lady is fairly serious, then she might request a separation. Normally, for blissful everyday life, both the accomplices must be faithful to one another

EARNESTNESS IS LIKEWISE EXCEPTIONALLY FUNDAMENTAL.

A lady likes it when her significant other showers love on her and cause her to feel that she is the main lady in his life. He should respond his sentiments towards her

•A DECENT SPOUSE SHOULD BE DEPENDABLE.

He should deal with his family, accommodate the kids' schooling and well-being and furthermore guarantee that his significant other is in capable hands financially and genuinely

•HE SHOULD FIND ACTUAL SUCCESS AT HIS VOCATION

His life partner may not see the value a not in a man show any outcome in his authority adventures. Each lady maintains that her significant other should find success, as progress implies flourishing to her loved ones

•Most lady regard an upstanding and genuine man. They like when their men try sincerely and demonstrate that they are fruitful.

•His confidence should be high. He should feel better about himself, and afterward just his significant other will likewise regard him

•

HE SHOULD BE A DECENT AUDIENCE

Most likely, a spouse has had a hard days work and anticipates that his better half should pay attention to him. At the equivalent, the spouse additionally had a similarly difficult stretch with family errands and youngsters to deal with and would like her better half to pay attention to her hardships. There must be a compromise relationship

•

FLEXIBILITY

A spouse should have the option to adjust to some random circumstance. He should have the option to commit time to the childhood of his kids and furthermore give satisfactory consideration to his better half's requirements. He should have the option to deal with family and family monetary emergencies

RESPONSIVENESS

A spouse who is delicate towards his significant other's sentiments is very much appreciated. A spouse needs all the profound and monetary help to raise her youngsters. She, all things considered, invests aloof energy taking care of the kids. Normally, she would anticipate that her significant other should be thoughtful towards her sentiments

It is clearly an ideal spouse must have a ton of good person characteristics which will make his significant other like and regard him. On the off chance that he is dependable, his significant other can likewise take great consideration of her loved ones.

REINFORCING THE FAMILY:

A couple have a serious obligation to cherish and really focus on one another and for their kids. … Guardians have a holy obligation to raise their youngsters in adoration and uprightness, to accommodate their physical and otherworldly necessities, to train them to cherish and serve each other, to notice the charges of God and to be reputable residents any place they live."

LOVE AND SOLIDARITY

I have long felt that joy in marriage isn't such a lot of a question of sentiment as it is a restless worry for the solace and prosperity of one's sidekick.

"The mystery of a blissful marriage is to serve God and one another. The objective of marriage is solidarity and unity, as well as self-improvement. Strangely, the more we serve each other, the more prominent is our profound and close to home development.

Solidarity in marriage doesn't come consequently or without exertion. Heartfelt love should develop into a pledge to look for and support profound concordance in marriage. Accomplishing conjugal solidarity takes gigantic tolerance and constancy and a reasonable vision of what our needs are in this life.

NONE ELSE

The words none else kill everybody and everything. The mate then, at that point, becomes superior in the existence of the husband or wife, and neither public activity nor word related life nor political life nor some other interest nor individual nor thing will at any point outweigh the friend companion. A spouse or wife who places kids, companions, vocations or leisure activities, before the conjugal relationship is in direct infringement of the rule "none else.

Not entirely set in stone to drive wedges of disunity between marriage accomplices. On the off chance that he can persuade one accomplice or the other that something different ought to outweigh this focal relationship of both time and endlessness, he has won a fight in his conflict against the family and against God's arrangement. We should thus accept unique consideration to assemble, support, and extend the marriage.

A DIFFICULT EXERCISE

Being a committed marriage accomplice and a cherishing, loyal parent is a fragile difficult exercise.

Guardians have a heavenly energize to bring [their] kids in light and truth. In any case, that obligation can turn out to be so tedious and sincerely requesting that now and again, on the off chance that moms and fathers are not careful, it can override or try and obstruct the marriage. To help marriage accomplices keep their familial needs all together, youngsters who experience childhood in the reflected sparkle of a caring marriage partake it could be said of safety that is in many cases missing when different worries are permitted to obscure that essential relationship. Married couples, who love one another, will observe that adoration and devotion are responded. This affection will give a sustaining environment to the close to home development of youngsters.

KIDS NEED LOVE AND RECOGNITION

Our youngsters need love and consideration, not extravagance; they need compassion and grasping, not apathy, from moms and fathers. They need the guardians' time. A mother's generous lessons and her affection for and trust in a young child or girl can in a real sense save them from a fiendish world. Acclaim your kids more than you right them," he directed. "Acclaim them for even their littlest accomplishment. … Urge your kids to come to you with their concerns and inquiries by paying attention to them consistently.

MY SUPPLICATION … is a request to save the kids. An excessive number of them stroll with torment and dread, in depression and sadness. Kids need daylight.

They need thoughtfulness and reward and warmth. Each home, no matter what the expense of the house, can give a climate of affection which will be a climate of salvation.

CHAPTER 24

COUPLE RELATIONSHIP DURING PREGNANCY

Pregnancy will achieve a ton of changes in your body and in your life. It can influence you both genuinely and intellectually. During pregnancy, while you figure out how to arrangement (and attempt to embrace) with the actual changes in your body, you will likewise need to manage the psychological pressure that you will take for reasons unknown. The more awful, Pregnancy chemicals, actual changes, or mental pressure can influence your marriage and the bond that you share with your accomplice.

By and by, it is fundamental that your accomplice knows and steady of your sentiments the whole time. This article will assist you comprehend how your relationship with spouse could change during pregnancy. It likewise offers a few hints which you can follow to keep a sound connection with your accomplice.

HOW DOES PREGNANCY CHANGE THE CONNECTION BETWEEN A COUPLE

You might have had an unshakable marriage up to this point, with zero battles, contentions or even grimaces. Yet, don't expect the norm to be something very similar during pregnancy. Pregnancy can influence your

RELATIONSHIP WITH YOUR BETTER HALF IN THE ACCOMPANYING WAYS

Your significant other or accomplice may be similarly however restless or focused as you may be, particularly in the event that you don't convey your necessities to him. These sentiments can prompt close to home distance and an absence of closeness.

The chemicals flowing through your body make close to home side-impacts, like apprehension, uneasiness, and neurosis. Numerous ladies start to counter these feelings by becoming tenacious and constraining their expressions of warmth on the spouse.

•Your sex drive will be in motion, yet assuming you feel drained, sick, and nauseous when your significant other attempts to start lovemaking, he could feel dismissed or let somewhere near you. This could encourage stoppage things between both of you.

The elements around you will radically change during your pregnancy. You could turn out to be more contemplative or outgoing, adjusting how your family and spouse view you as a necessary piece of their lives.

During pregnancy, actual changes in your body will be apparent. You will likewise have stretch imprints, varicose veins, body hair, etc, and all of this can upset you and make you hesitant. While your significant other may in any case imagine that you are the most gorgeous lady and need to invest some heartfelt energy with you, in the event that you don't feel something very similar, you probably shouldn't partake in some heartfelt time. As a matter of fact, it could cause a crack in the sexual science you once shared.

ABRAHAM SHRUB

CHAPTER 25

WHY IS IT CRITICAL TO KEEP A DECENT CONNECTION BETWEEN A SPOUSE AND HUSBAND DURING PREGNANCY?

You and your companion should be most likely subsided into the solace of routine with one another. Your regular obligations are simpler when shared. The security of returning home to somebody who will show up for you is something many individuals want. Furthermore, when you become pregnant, the obligations and nerves expansion in equivalent measure. Sharing these weights will be both useful and smart for yourself as well as your child. Consider how your lives are going to change and go with the choices that are ideal for the little one that is soon to get back home.

TIPS TO KEEP THE RELATIONSHIP SOLID WHILE PREGNANT

The following are a few hints on keeping up with your relationship and how to be a strong spouse during pregnancy -

GET PREPARED FOR THE CHILD TOGETHER

Having a child implies much more work for both of you after birth. You can plan ahead of time in numerous ways. This incorporates making a resting region for the infant, either in your room or in a different nursery, purchasing nappies, milk bottles, child garments, pacifiers, covers, cushions, toys, lodgings and countless other fundamental things. Doing these errands together will assist the new dad with feeling needed and responsible for child choices than in any case.

PUT TIME AWAY FOR ONE ANOTHER

Pregnancy implies unending regular checkups, weariness, stress, and profound distance with your accomplice. Yet, these issues shouldn't let you down or influence your relationship. Ensure that you invest sufficient energy with your life partner and impart unreservedly about one another requirements. This will forestall both of you from lacking consideration or closeness, reinforcing your bond.

KEEP UP WITH THE CLOSENESS

Try not to let the flash of sentiment vanish. Pregnancy changes will make them feel swelled, drained and surly. Be that as it may, it is significant you go out with your companion consistently, even on heartfelt dates. It very well may be pretty much as essential as requesting food home and watching a film while nestling together.

. SELECT A CHILD NAME

This is a significant one. The name you decide for your kid will in all probability accompany him until the end of his lives. Take a stab at searching for the right name together. Invest energy with your accomplice and choose a name for your child that you both like and concur upon. You could pick a name that is influential for both of you, so neither needs to understand left.

•

VISIT THE SPECIALIST TOGETHER

Go with your accomplice for all your medical checkups. Both of you will get direct data about the child's advancement like weight, well-being, as well as future strides in the pregnancy. Fathers who include themselves at this stage will generally be more associated with the entire cycle, and subsequently more engaged with the pregnancy and the relationship.

CHAPTER 26

HOW SEX CAN FORTIFY CONNECTIONS: THE ADVANTAGES OF HAVING INTERCOURSE ON A MORE REGULAR BASIS

HOW TRULY DOES SEX INFLUENCE A RELATIONSHIP

Quality sex in a strong relationship is connected to all encompassing medical advantages as well as cultural advantages. Standard closeness has assisted bring down the separation with rating and relationship crumbling consistently.

With regards to its immediate consequences for the gatherings in question, for example monogamous accomplices, the accompanying can reinforce the case that sex can fortify connections:

SEX REINFORCES THE ASSOCIATION BETWEEN COUPLES

The closeness made and experienced during monogamous sex reinforces profound association, bond, and responsibility. It keeps a sound degree of closeness, love, and belonging, which people need normally according to Maslow's Order of Requirements.

Sex can fortify a relationship by keeping up with the "flash." It saves the craving to remain together despite life's battles.

Closeness as sex likewise lays out and reinforces an encouraging group of people, in particular your accomplice. Individuals who have a decent encouraging group of people will generally have the option to frame significant connections and oversee pressure better.

SEXUAL FULFILLMENT LIFTS STATE OF MIND AND BLISS

Deductively talking, does sex reinforce a relationship? The response is yes.

Essentially, the less focused on you are, the more joyful and more happy your perspective.

As far as one might be concerned, climax sets off the arrival of the chemical prolactin. While its primary capability benefits lactation, it additionally advances great rest and unwinding. Furthermore, a very much refreshed body is more equipped for supporting physical and social connections.

Sex is likewise a pressure the executives method. It lessens the emission of the survival chemicals, cortisol and adrenaline, which both make physiological pressure reactions like depletion and expanded circulatory strain.

The mind likewise delivers endorphins or lighthearted synthetics during sex. These improve mind-set and lessen sensations of dejection and crabbiness.

One more substance is delivered with additional sexual excitement. It's called oxytocin, and it makes a feeling of fulfillment and serenity.

What is oxytocin? It is a peptide chemical created by the nerve center and emitted by the back pituitary for sexual holding and labor.

SEXUAL COMMUNICATION FURTHER DEVELOPS REGARD AND MENTAL SELF VIEW

Certainty increments with sexual fulfillment. This is on the grounds that sex helps support one's confidence.

This, thusly, can make a decent and solid effect on friendly and close connections.

As referenced previously, sex achieves closeness through expanded measures of oxytocin. It satisfies a piece of the human psychological condition.

Sex fosters the longing to snuggle, the desire to bond with the other individual, and the need to hold one more and be held by another.

. SEX MAKES IMMEDIACY IN THE RELATIONSHIP

How significant is sex in a drawn out relationship, you inquire?

There's generally a feeling of fervor when there's a genuinely new thing to anticipate. A similar idea applies to sex.

Brightening up your affection life in the room helps add energy and sentiment in a relationship. It consoles couples of their obligation to one another.

IT RESTORES SENTIMENTS AND REVIVES SENTIMENT

Hitched life can get going and requesting with the numerous obligations laid on the way — work, bringing up youngsters, monetary commitments, well-being concerns, individual time, settling on choices gainful and reasoning for all relatives, among others. Revived love is among the many advantages of sex in marriage and in long haul connections.

Sex can reinforce connections by empowering two gatherings to effectively take part in a caring movement, regardless of the feverish timetables and burdening tasks. It reconnects two individuals and takes them back to the revelation stage, permitting them to become both as people and as accomplices throughout everyday life.

Make time to engage in sexual relations. Flash the drive by:

•Encouraging closeness even external the room. Plan date evenings. Work on projects together.

•Talking about significant issues, for example how you can have better sex, what's holding you back from having an interest, and so forth. Distinguish and dispense with stressors. Open correspondence is the way to fulfillment in the room.

•Getting tech gadgets far from the bed. Limit the utilization of your cell phone. Put the television controller a ways off.

CHAPTER 27

PRESENT NEW IMPROVEMENTS. ATTEMPT NEW EXERCISES, POSITIONS, AND TOYS. EXPLORE!

WHY IS SEX SO SIGNIFICANT IN A RELATIONSHIP?

By discussing sex and by really having intercourse, accomplices impart transparently and compromise all the more successfully. Better. Consensual (and energetic) Commonly assented sex, as it were, tweaks the omissions and holes in connections.

Be that as it may, the advantages of sex go past feelings and mind. It has its own setup of well-being advantages.

A public report executed through the organization of delegates from Michigan State College and the College of Chicago detailed that collaborated sexuality is connected to bring down dangers of cardiovascular circumstances in more seasoned ladies.

Another review: distributed first distributed in the clinical diary Psych neuroendocrinology lead to a starter end that ordinary sexual closeness can draw out life. Long telomeres were found in the female subjects who detailed sexual movement throughout the review.

What are telomeres? These are DNA strand defenders. The more drawn out these are for all intents and purposes, the less the probability of biting the dust youthful or fostering a degenerative condition.

Other announced medical advantages of sex include:

- Lower hazard of malignant growth, particularly in the regenerative and endocrine frameworks
- Increments torment limit
- Better resistance
- Further developed bladder control
- Fills in as exercise

HOW FREQUENTLY WOULD IT BE A GOOD IDEA FOR YOU TO HAVE INTERCOURSE?

Americans in their 20s will generally have intercourse at a normal of 80 times each year by and large; Americans in their 60s do it at a normal of 20 times each year. These information were drawn from a review distributed in the Chronicles of Sexual Way of behaving in 2017.

Yet, could we at any point consider these frequencies solid?

As per a Review : done at the Kinsey Establishment in Indiana, quality is a higher priority than amount with regards to sex. The justifications for why one takes part in sex is undeniably more significant — relationship fulfillment, bliss, and better closeness ought to be the center results.

Positive relational communications, for example, sex and friendship are fundamental for human prosperity. All the more in this way, they can reinforce connections.

In this way, make sure to how you can be more joyful and more satisfied between the sheets with your accomplice. It'll move the heartfelt energies along and the fervor alive.

CHAPTER 28

REASONS THAT LEAD TO CONTENTIONS BETWEEN A TO-BE-MOTHER AND A TO-BE-FATHER

The following are some relationship issues during pregnancy that could prompt battles among you and your accomplice. However, don't stress since, in such a case that you and your accomplice contend in view of the accompanying reasons, we have a few hints to stop the issue from really developing.

NONATTENDANCE OF CONSIDERATION FROM THE ACCOMPLICE

Issue: The physical and profound changes during pregnancy can prompt an expanded feeling of weakness and instability. During this time, you could feel that your accomplice isn't furnishing you with enough consideration or care. This could prompt disagreements.

Arrangement: Being excessively difficult about minor subtleties like missing physical checkups could make your accomplice less anxious to go with you the following time. You could ask your loved ones to contribute when your significant other isn't anywhere near.

FAMILY SHOW

Issue - Every one of the four of your folks should get more engaged with your pregnancy to the degree of needing to control all parts of your life. This could be an issue on the off chance that there is ridiculous analysis tossed at you or your accomplice.

Arrangement - It means a lot to work this out with your accomplice. You both are the ones having a child and the choices must be yours alone. While family support is fundamental, guarantee their impedance doesn't influence your day to day routine or your relationship with your accomplice.

MONETARY ISSUES

Issue - Children are costly - assuming you gone for even a couple of your clinical arrangements so for, you realize that it's valid. The bills begin mounting with pregnancy clinical consideration, pre-birth diet and physical checkups, etc. This quick expansion in the financial plan can be intellectually burdening, which can prompt contentions among you and your accomplice.

Arrangement - Work through it together. Plan a feasible financial plan, regardless of whether it implies disposing of undesirable costs. Try not to hold on until the child is destined to do this, as you will absolutely not have time then, at that point.

ABSENCE OF SEXUAL CLOSENESS

Issue: As referenced previously, with the extraordinary actual changes your body during pregnancy, sex may be keep going at the forefront of your thoughts. However, that may not be no different for your accomplice - he will in any case be drawn to you and should engage in sexual relations with you. In any case, on the off chance that you are not ready, it could cause him to feel undesired.

Arrangement: rather than quarreling over it, attempts and check out at the lighter side of things. You may not feel hot when you have such a lot of gas in your midsection or need to pee constantly. The key isn't to view yourself so pretentiously. On the off chance that sex isn't on the plate, take a stab at nestling or being comfortable with your accomplice.

YOUNGSTER NAMES

Issue - Child naming is a significant holding process for the guardians. However, conflicts are normal over this issue, and they can bring about out and out battles.

Arrangement - You could despise naming your child after his granddad and he could reject your decision of name for being excessively strange. The arrangement is straightforward: Continue onward at it. The rundown of potential child names is perpetual; you simply need to look through till you find one you are both content with. Additionally, this isn't the main thing about your child that you should think twice about.

Does a Battle or a Contention Among A couple Influence the Youngster in the Belly?

Notwithstanding the ones previously referenced, there are different reasons for contentions and battles between pregnant couples. You won't understand when you begin contending with your accomplice during pregnancy and maybe fault your pregnancy chemicals, each time you do. Be that as it may, if it's not too much trouble, think long and hard about you start a verbal fight with your accomplice as your little one will tune in. A portion of the manners by which battles among a couple during pregnancy influence the unborn youngster are:

•Significant stretches of pressure can prompt side effects of gloom and nervousness in both the mother and the child. It can additionally bring about unsuccessful labor, unexpected labor or stillbirth.

- Infants brought into the world under distressing circumstances can have unexpected problems like low birth weight, etc.

•Stress can likewise prompt an expansion in circulatory strain and hormonal irregularity, which can likewise cause premature delivery and preterm work.

•Pregnancy tension has been known to expand the dangers of post pregnancy anxiety, which is risky to both your well-being and your child's well-being as well.

Pregnancy can prompt personal disturbance influencing your bond with your accomplice. You really must focus on any potential triggers that could bring about a battle, in order to shield your child's prosperity. Comprehend that the two accomplices play their own parts to play in this gorgeous cycle, despite the fact that they have alternate points of view. Accommodate your disparities and fabricate a more grounded, better starting point for your new excursion of life as a parent.

www.ingramcontent.com/pod-product-compliance
Lightning Source LLC
LaVergne TN
LVHW012116170826
845678LV00014BA/2960

9798849270333